INTEGRATING
Ancient Civilizations
with Reading Instruction

6 Complete Social Studies Units

Written by
Trisha Callella

Editor: LaDawn Walter
Illustrator: Jenny Campbell
Cover Illustrator: Rick Grayson
Designer/Production: Moonhee Pak/Terri Lamadrid
Cover Designer: Moonhee Pak
Art Director: Tom Cochrane
Project Director: Carolea Williams

Table of Contents

Introduction

For many students, reading comprehension diminishes when they read nonfiction text. Students often have difficulty understanding social studies vocabulary, making inferences, and grasping social studies concepts. With so much curriculum to cover each day, social studies content is sometimes put on the back burner when it comes to academic priorities. *Integrating Ancient Civilizations with Reading Instruction* provides the perfect integration of social studies content with specific reading instruction to help students improve their comprehension of nonfiction text and maximize every minute of your teaching day.

This resource includes six units that are related to ancient civilizations. The units are based on the most common social studies topics taught in sixth grade in accordance with the national social studies standards:

Mesopotamia   **Olmec Civilization**
Mummies of Egypt   **Greek Gods and Goddesses**
The Great Wall of China   **Gladiators of Rome**

Each unit includes powerful prereading strategies, such as predicting what the story will be about, accessing prior knowledge, and brainstorming about vocabulary that may be included in the reading selection. Following the prereading exercises is a nonfiction reading selection written on a sixth grade reading level. Each reading selection is followed by essential postreading activities such as comprehension questions on multiple taxonomy levels, skill reviews, and a critical thinking exercise. Each unit also includes a hands-on activity that connects each social studies topic to students' lives. The descriptions on pages 5–8 include the objectives and implementation strategies for each unit component.

Before, during, and after reading the story, students are exposed to the same reading strategies you typically reinforce during your language arts instruction block and guided reading. This powerful duo gives you the opportunity to teach both reading and social studies simultaneously. Using the activities in this resource, students will continue *learning to read* while *reading to learn*. They will become more successful readers while gaining new social studies knowledge and experiences.

Prereading Strategies

✓ Catch a Clue
✓ Concept Map
✓ Word Warm-Up

Nonfiction Text

Postreading Applications

✓ Comprehension Questions
✓ Sharpen Your Skills
✓ Get Logical

Hands-on Social Studies

Connections to Standards

This chart shows the concepts that are covered in each unit based on the national social studies standards.

	Mesopotamia	Mummies of Egypt	The Great Wall of China	Olmec Civilization	Greek Gods and Goddesses	Gladiators of Rome
Compare and contrast differences about past events, people, places, or situations, and identify how they contribute to understanding the past.	●	●	●	●	●	●
Identify and describe selected historical periods and patterns of change within and across cultures.	●	●	●	●	●	●
Develop critical sensitivities such as empathy and skepticism regarding attitudes, values, and behaviors of people in different historical contexts.	●	●	●	●	●	●
Relate personal changes to social, cultural, and historical contexts.	●	●	●	●	●	●
Describe personal connections to places such as community, nation, and world.	●	●	●	●	●	●
Work independently and cooperatively to accomplish goals.	●	●	●	●	●	●
Explain conditions, actions, and motivations that contribute to conflict and cooperation within and among nations.	●	●	●	●	●	●
Give examples of conflict, cooperation, and interdependence among individuals, groups, and nations.	●	●	●	●	●	●
Investigate concerns, issues, standards, and conflicts related to universal human rights such as religious groups and the effects of war.		●	●		●	●
Describe ways that language, stories, and artistic creations are expressions of culture and influence behavior of people living in a particular culture.	●	●	●	●	●	●

Unit Overview

Catch a Clue

<u>Objectives</u>

Students will

✓ be introduced to key concepts and vocabulary *before* reading

✓ be able to transfer this key strategy to improve test-taking skills

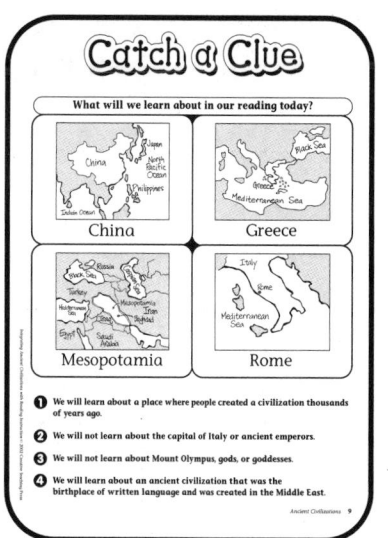

<u>Implementation</u>

Students will use clues and the process of elimination to predict what the nonfiction reading selection will be about. Copy this page on an overhead transparency, and use it for a whole-class activity. Begin by reading aloud each word, and ask students to repeat the words. Read the clues one at a time. Then, discuss with the class what topic(s) could be eliminated and the reasons why. (Note: There will be clues that do not eliminate any topics. The purpose of this is to teach students that although there is information listed, it is not always helpful information.) Cross off a topic when the class decides that it does not fit the clues. If there is more than one topic left after the class discusses all of the clues, this becomes a prediction activity. When this occurs, reread the clues with the class, and discuss which answer would be most appropriate given the clues provided.

Concept Map

<u>Objectives</u>

Students will

✓ access prior knowledge by brainstorming what they already know about the topic

✓ increase familiarity with the social studies content by hearing others' prior knowledge experiences

✓ revisit the map *after* reading to recall information from the reading selection

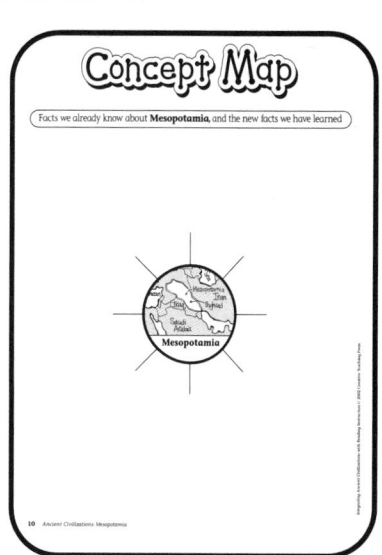

<u>Implementation</u>

Copy this page on an overhead transparency, and use it for a whole-class activity. Use a colored pen to write students' prior knowledge on the transparency. After the class reads the story, use a different colored pen to add what students learned.

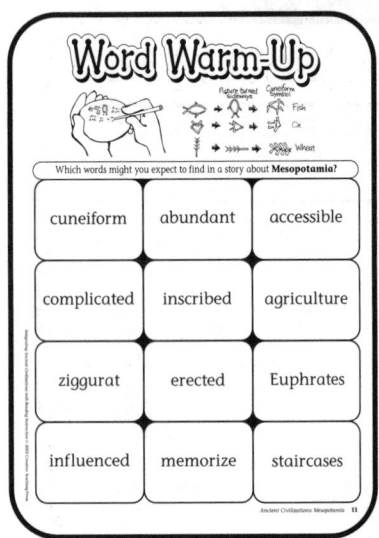

Word Warm-Up

Objectives

Students will

✓ be introduced to new vocabulary words

✓ make predictions about the story using thinking and reasoning skills

✓ begin to monitor their own comprehension

Implementation

Students will use the strategy of exclusion brainstorming to identify which words are likely to be in the story and which words are unrelated and should be eliminated from the list. Copy this page on an overhead transparency, and use it for a whole-class activity. Have students make predictions about which of the vocabulary words could be in the story and which words probably would not be in the story. Ask them to give reasons for their predictions. For example, say *Do you think staircases would be in a story about Mesopotamia?* A student may say *Yes, because they made ziggurats that looked like staircases* or *No, because staircases are in tall buildings, which were not made then.* Circle the word if a student says that it will be in the story, and cross it out if a student says it will not be in the story. Do not correct students' responses. After reading, students can either confirm or disconfirm their own predictions. It is more powerful for students to verify their predictions on their own than to be told the answer before ever reading the story.

Nonfiction Text

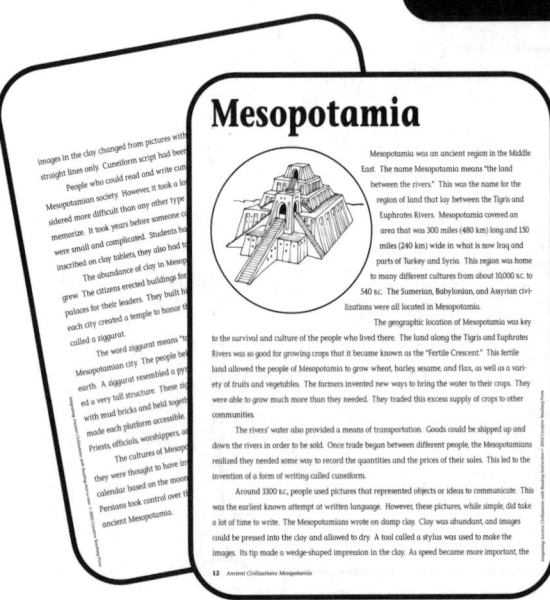

The Story

Objectives

Students will

✓ read high-interest, nonfiction stories

✓ increase social studies knowledge

✓ increase content area vocabulary

✓ connect social studies facts with their own experiences

Implementation

Give each student a copy of the story, and display the corresponding Word Warm-Up transparency while you read the story with the class. After the class reads the story, go back to the transparency, and have students discuss their predictions in relation to the new information they learned in the story. Invite students to identify any changes they would make on the transparency and give reasons for their responses. Then, revisit the corresponding Concept Map transparency, and write the new information students have learned.

Postreading Applications

Comprehension Questions

Objectives

Students will

✓ recall factual information

✓ be challenged to think beyond the story facts to make inferences

✓ connect the story to other reading, their own lives, and the world around them

Implementation

Use these questions to facilitate a class discussion of the story. Choose the number and types of questions that best meet the abilities of your class.

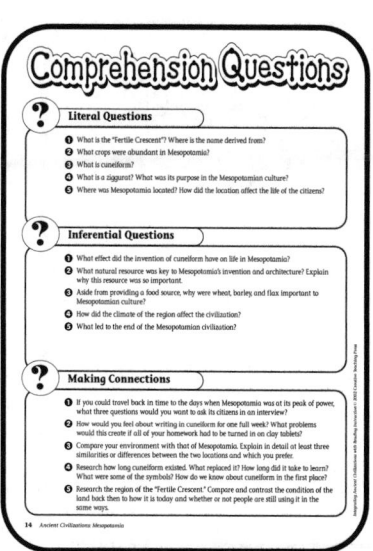

Sharpen Your Skills

Objectives

Students will

✓ practice answering questions in common test-taking formats

✓ integrate language arts skills with social studies knowledge

Implementation

After the class reads a story, give each student a copy of this page. Ask students to read each question and all of the answer choices for that question before deciding on an answer. Show them how to use their pencil to completely fill in the circle for their answer. Invite students to raise their hand if they have difficulty reading a question and/or the answer choices. Thoroughly explain the types of questions and exactly what is being asked the first few times students use this reproducible.

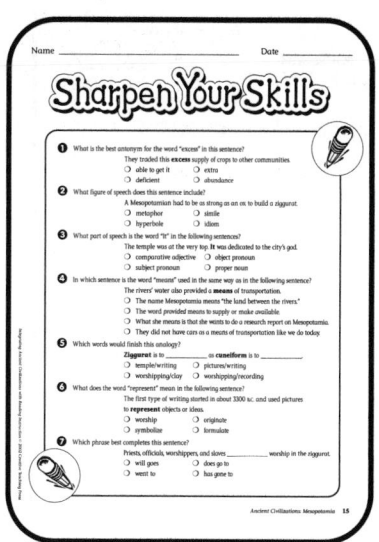

Get Logical

Objectives

Students will

✓ practice logical and strategic thinking skills

✓ practice the skill of process of elimination

✓ transfer the information read by applying it to new situations

Implementation

Give each student a copy of this page. Read the beginning sentences and the clues to familiarize students with the words. Show students step-by-step how to eliminate choices based on the clues given. Have students place an X in a box that represents an impossible choice, thereby narrowing down the options for accurate choices. Once students understand the concept, they can work independently on this reproducible.

Hands-on Social Studies

Social Studies Activity

Objectives

Students will

✓ participate in hands-on learning experiences

✓ expand and reinforce social studies knowledge

✓ apply new social studies vocabulary words

Implementation

The social studies activities in this book incorporate a variety of skills students are required to experience at this age level (e.g., survey, interview, analyze, evaluate). Each hands-on activity begins with an explanation of its purpose to help direct the intended learning. Give each student a copy of any corresponding reproducibles and/or materials for the activity. Then, introduce the activity and explain the directions. Model any directions that may be difficult for students to follow on their own.

Catch a Clue

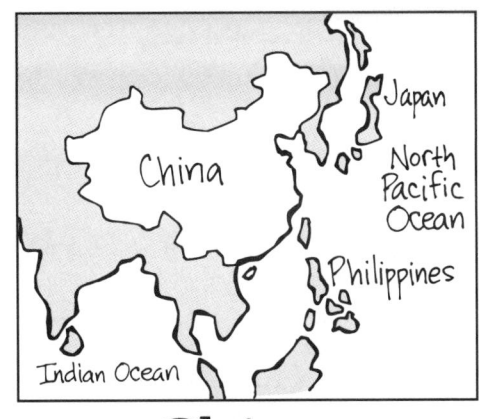

China

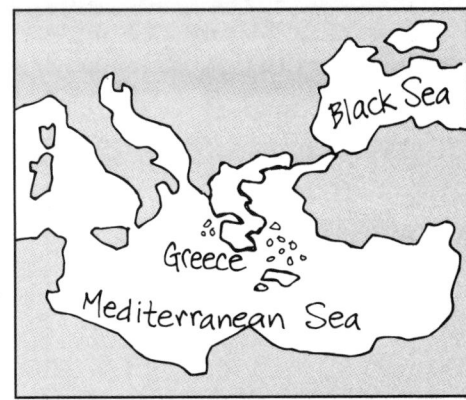

Greece

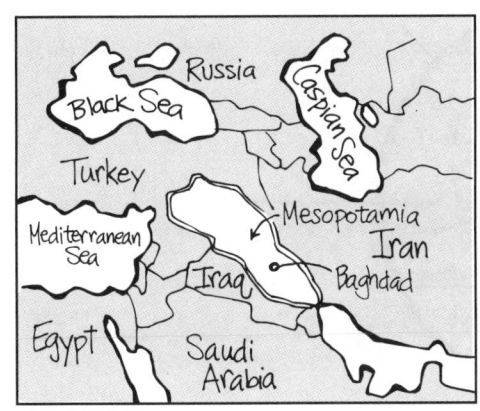

Mesopotamia

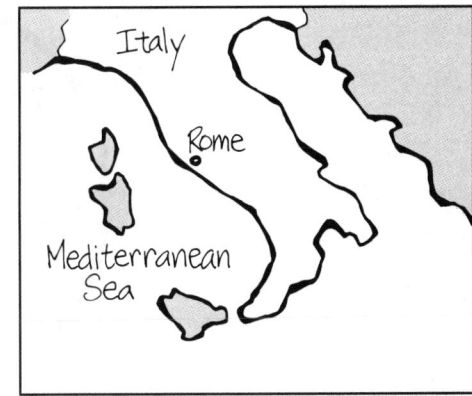

Rome

1 We will learn about a place where people created a civilization thousands of years ago.

2 We will not learn about the capital of Italy or ancient emperors.

3 We will not learn about Mount Olympus, gods, or goddesses.

4 We will learn about an ancient civilization that was the birthplace of written language and was created in the Middle East.

Concept Map

Facts we already know about **Mesopotamia,** and the new facts we have learned

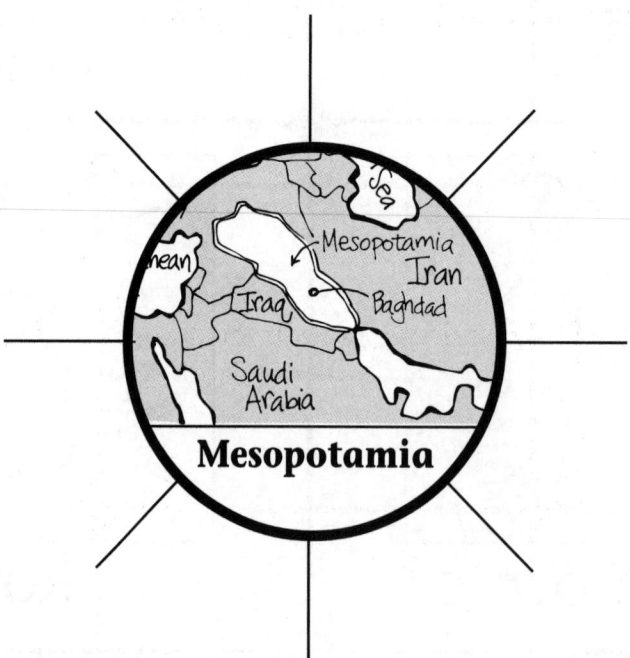

Mesopotamia

Integrating Ancient Civilizations with Reading Instruction © 2002 Creative Teaching Press

Word Warm-Up

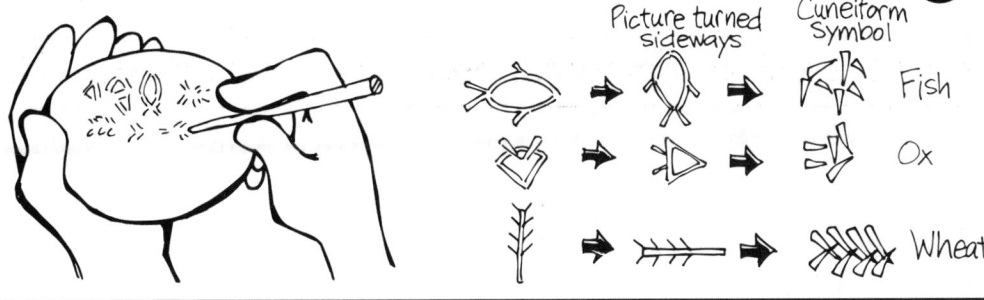

Picture turned sideways | Cuneiform Symbol

Fish

Ox

Wheat

Which words might you expect to find in a story about **Mesopotamia?**

cuneiform	abundant	accessible
complicated	inscribed	agriculture
ziggurat	erected	Euphrates
influenced	memorize	staircases

Mesopotamia

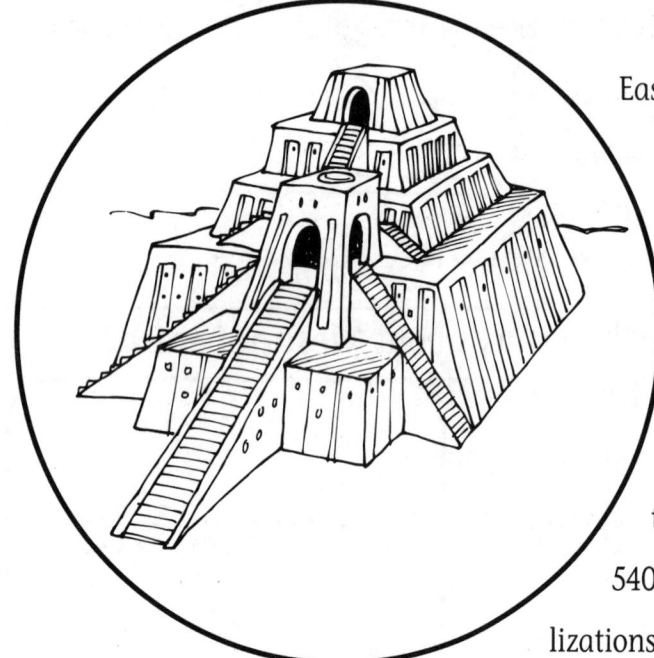

Mesopotamia was an ancient region in the Middle East. The name Mesopotamia means "the land between the rivers." This was the name for the region of land that lay between the Tigris and Euphrates Rivers. Mesopotamia covered an area that was 300 miles (480 km) long and 150 miles (240 km) wide in what is now Iraq and parts of Turkey and Syria. This region was home to many different cultures from about 10,000 B.C. to 540 B.C. The Sumerian, Babylonian, and Assyrian civilizations were all located in Mesopotamia.

The geographic location of Mesopotamia was key to the survival and culture of the people who lived there. The land along the Tigris and Euphrates Rivers was so good for growing crops that it became known as the "Fertile Crescent." This fertile land allowed the people of Mesopotamia to grow wheat, barley, sesame, and flax, as well as a variety of fruits and vegetables. The farmers invented new ways to bring the water to their crops. They were able to grow much more than they needed. They traded this excess supply of crops to other communities.

The rivers' water also provided a means of transportation. Goods could be shipped up and down the rivers in order to be sold. Once trade began between different people, the Mesopotamians realized they needed some way to record the quantities and the prices of their sales. This led to the invention of a form of writing called cuneiform.

Around 3300 B.C., people used pictures that represented objects or ideas to communicate. This was the earliest known attempt at written language. However, these pictures, while simple, did take a lot of time to write. The Mesopotamians wrote on damp clay. Clay was abundant, and images could be pressed into the clay and allowed to dry. A tool called a stylus was used to make the images. Its tip made a wedge-shaped impression in the clay. As speed became more important, the

Integrating Ancient Civilizations with Reading Instruction © 2002 Creative Teaching Press

images in the clay changed from pictures with curved lines to those forms that could be made with straight lines only. Cuneiform script had been invented.

People who could read and write cuneiform script were very important in the Mesopotamian society. However, it took a long time to learn how to do this. At the time, it was considered more difficult than any other type of work. There were more than 500 different signs to memorize. It took years before someone could properly learn all of these signs. Cuneiform signs were small and complicated. Students had to learn how to write neatly. Because the signs were inscribed on clay tablets, they also had to write without making mistakes.

The abundance of clay in Mesopotamia also provided an ideal building material as the cities grew. The citizens erected buildings for their homes and to house their government. They built palaces for their leaders. They built high walls for protection from floods and attacks. In addition, each city created a temple to honor their gods. This temple would be built on top of a structure called a ziggurat.

The word ziggurat means "to build high." Ziggurats were the center of religious life in every Mesopotamian city. The people believed that the ziggurat was the connection between heaven and earth. A ziggurat resembled a pyramid-shaped tower with a series of stacked platforms that created a very tall structure. These ziggurats were between three and seven tiers high. They were built with mud bricks and held together with wood beams and reed matting. Ramps and staircases made each platform accessible. The temple was at the very top. It was dedicated to the city's god. Priests, officials, worshippers, and slaves were always coming and going from this great structure.

The cultures of Mesopotamia were great in their day. Besides cuneiform and the ziggurats, they were thought to have invented the wheel, used mathematics, developed maps, and developed a calendar based on the moon's phases. Eventually, the power of Mesopotamia began to fade as the Persians took control over the region. However, to this day, we benefit from the contributions of ancient Mesopotamia.

Integrating Ancient Civilizations with Reading Instruction © 2002 Creative Teaching Press

Comprehension Questions

❓ Literal Questions

1. What is the "Fertile Crescent"? Where is the name derived from?
2. What crops were abundant in Mesopotamia?
3. What is cuneiform?
4. What is a ziggurat? What was its purpose in the Mesopotamian culture?
5. Where was Mesopotamia located? How did the location affect the life of the citizens?

❓ Inferential Questions

1. What effect did the invention of cuneiform have on life in Mesopotamia?
2. What natural resource was key to Mesopotamia's invention and architecture? Explain why this resource was so important.
3. Aside from providing a food source, why were wheat, barley, and flax important to Mesopotamian culture?
4. How did the climate of the region affect the civilization?
5. What led to the end of the Mesopotamian civilization?

❓ Making Connections

1. If you could travel back in time to the days when Mesopotamia was at its peak of power, what three questions would you want to ask its citizens in an interview?
2. How would you feel about writing in cuneiform for one full week? What problems would this create if all of your homework had to be turned in on clay tablets?
3. Compare your environment with that of Mesopotamia. Explain in detail at least three similarities or differences between the two locations and which you prefer.
4. Research how long cuneiform existed. What replaced it? How long did it take to learn? What were some of the symbols? How do we know about cuneiform in the first place?
5. Research the region of the "Fertile Crescent." Compare and contrast the condition of the land back then to how it is today and whether or not people are still using it in the same ways.

Integrating Ancient Civilizations with Reading Instruction © 2002 Creative Teaching Press

Sharpen Your Skills

1 What is the best antonym for the word "excess" in this sentence?

They traded this **excess** supply of crops to other communities.
- ○ able to get it
- ○ extra
- ○ deficient
- ○ abundance

2 What figure of speech does this sentence include?

A Mesopotamian had to be as strong as an ox to build a ziggurat.
- ○ metaphor
- ○ simile
- ○ hyperbole
- ○ idiom

3 What part of speech is the word "It" in the following sentences?

The temple was at the very top. **It** was dedicated to the city's god.
- ○ comparative adjective
- ○ object pronoun
- ○ subject pronoun
- ○ proper noun

4 In which sentence is the word "means" used in the same way as in the following sentence?

The rivers' water also provided a **means** of transportation.
- ○ The name Mesopotamia means "the land between the rivers."
- ○ The word *provided* means to supply or make available.
- ○ What she means is that she wants to do a research report on Mesopotamia.
- ○ They did not have cars as a means of transportation like we do today.

5 Which words would finish this analogy?

Ziggurat is to _____ as **cuneiform** is to _____.
- ○ temple/writing
- ○ pictures/writing
- ○ worshipping/clay
- ○ worshipping/recording

6 What does the word "represent" mean in the following sentence?

The first type of writing started in about 3300 B.C. and used pictures to **represent** objects or ideas.
- ○ worship
- ○ originate
- ○ symbolize
- ○ formulate

7 Which phrase best completes this sentence?

Priests, officials, worshippers, and slaves _____ worship in the ziggurat.
- ○ will goes
- ○ does go to
- ○ went to
- ○ has gone to

Get Logical

Mr. Rhode's class is split up into cooperative groups. Each group is responsible for creating one complete report on a topic related to ancient civilizations. Maddie, Jay, Jack, Marissa, and Ellie are in a group. They decided to create a report on Mesopotamia. Use the clues below to decide which aspect of Mesopotamian life each student was responsible for researching.

Clues

❶ Marissa's section did not include information about crops or the location of Mesopotamia.

❷ Neither Ellie nor Jay researched when Mesopotamia was home to many cultures.

❸ Neither Maddie, Marissa, or Ellie included information about the wheel, calendar, or math in her section.

❹ The information about the crops that were grown was not a part of the section written by Ellie, Jay, or Maddie.

❺ The information that included the description of the rivers, continent, countries, and climate was in Maddie's section of the research report.

	Maddie	Jay	Jack	Marissa	Ellie
Time Span					
Inventions					
Geography					
Agriculture					
Economics					

Maddie researched _____.

Jay researched _____.

Jack researched _____.

Marissa researched _____.

Ellie researched _____.

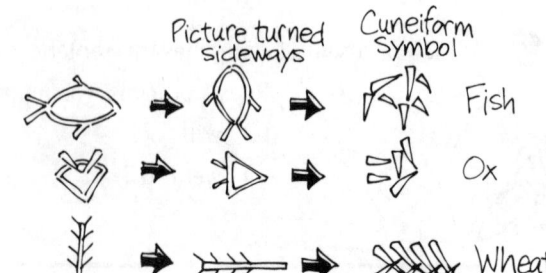

Picture turned sideways   Cuneiform Symbol

Fish

Ox

Wheat

Integrating Ancient Civilizations with Reading Instruction © 2002 Creative Teaching Press

Vegetable Garden

Purpose

The purpose of this activity is to help students understand the importance of planting and maintaining crops. Students will grow their own lettuce, radish, small carrot, or cilantro. Then, they will trade crops and make a salad.

MATERIALS

- ✔ Vegetable Garden Record Sheet (page 18)
- ✔ Vegetable Garden Reflections reproducible (page 19)
- ✔ buckets or plastic planters
- ✔ potting soil
- ✔ seeds (lettuce types, radish, small carrots, cilantro, other shallow root vegetables)
- ✔ masking tape
- ✔ permanent markers
- ✔ water
- ✔ rulers

Implementation

Explain to students that Mesopotamians were among the first people to grow crops in abundance and trade their excess for other items they wanted or needed. They were the first to make the leap from a hunting-and-gathering–based society to an agrarian-based society. Also, Mesopotamians soon set up a trade system based on agriculture and developed writing to keep their records of trade accurate. Pair up students for this activity if room or cost is a concern. Give each student a bucket or plastic planter, potting soil, one or more types of seeds, and a piece of tape. Have students write their name with a permanent marker on the tape and stick it to their bucket or planter. Ask students to fill their bucket with potting soil. Tell students to plant each item according to the planting guide on the seed package. Students can plant all of one or several kinds of vegetables. Place the buckets or planters in an area close to windows. Invite students to water their plants according to the directions on the seed package. Give each student several copies of the Vegetable Garden Record Sheet. Have students keep a daily record of their plants' progress. Ask them to record the date, any observations about the plant, and the height and/or width of the plant. (Have students use a ruler to determine this information.) When the vegetables reach maturity, invite students to trade their vegetables and make a salad. Invite students to eat the salad when it is done. Then, give each student a Vegetable Garden Reflections reproducible to complete.

_____'s

Vegetable Garden Record Sheet

Date	Observations	Plant Size

Integrating Ancient Civilizations with Reading Instruction © 2002 Creative Teaching Press

Name _____   Date _____

Vegetable Garden Reflections

Directions: After participating in the Vegetable Garden activity, answer the following questions.

1 What parts of growing a garden did you enjoy the most?

_____

_____

2 Which aspects were frustrating about growing the garden?

_____

_____

3 In what ways did you gain an appreciation for the early Mesopotamians and the work they did in growing crops?

_____

_____

4 In what ways were your farming methods similar to those of the early Mesopotamians?

_____

_____

5 In what ways were your farming methods different from those of the early Mesopotamians?

_____

_____

6 Will you attempt to grow a garden again on your own? _____ Why or why not?

_____

_____

Integrating Ancient Civilizations with Reading Instruction © 2002 Creative Teaching Press

Catch a Clue

What will we learn about in our reading today?

gladiators

Homer
Greek mythology

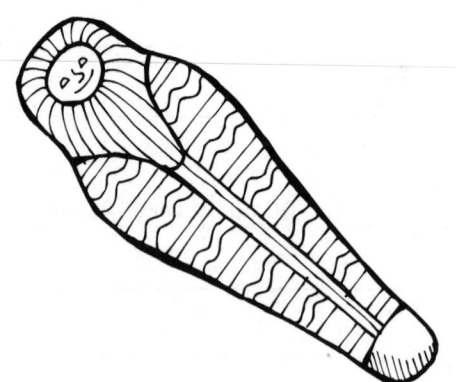

mummies of Egypt

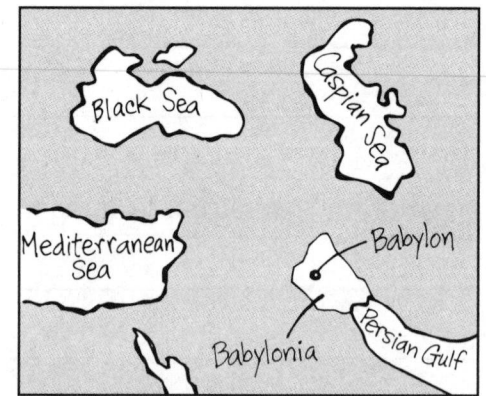

the Babylonians

1 We will not learn about deities that made their home on Mount Olympus.

2 The people of this area did not invest time in fighting.

3 We will learn more about a region that is south of Mesopotamia.

4 We will learn more about a young king and the beliefs of his time.

Integrating Ancient Civilizations with Reading Instruction © 2002 Creative Teaching Press

Concept Map

Facts we already know about **mummies of Egypt**, and the new facts we have learned

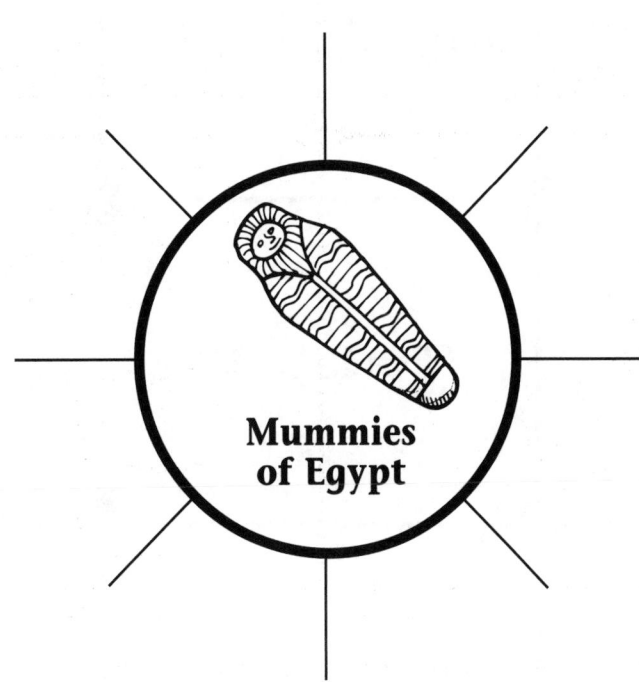

**Mummies
of Egypt**

Word Warm-Up

Which words might you expect to find in a story about **mummies of Egypt?**

embalming	superstitious	mummification
copper	treasures	furniture
internal	excavation	artifacts
archeology	ascended	concealed

Integrating Ancient Civilizations with Reading Instruction © 2002 Creative Teaching Press

Mummies of Egypt

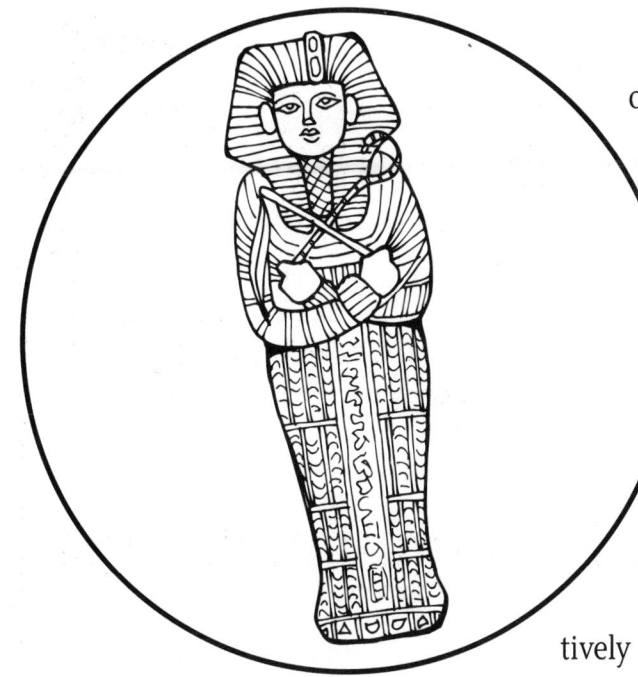

Between 1977 and 1979, the United States was honored to be part of a special event. An amazing exhibit, the "Treasures of Tutankhamen," toured major cities in the United States for the first time ever. This collection contained hundreds of artifacts from the country of Egypt. The collection was gathered from the most complete excavation of an Egyptian tomb ever made. The treasures of Tutankhamen were special.

Who was Tutankhamen? He was a relatively minor king of Egypt who reigned from about 1333 to 1323 B.C. King Tutankhamen, often known with affection as King Tut, was only nine years of age when he ascended the throne of the kingdom of Egypt. His reign was short. He died when he was only eighteen years old.

As far as Egyptian kings go, King Tut was not the wealthiest or the most powerful. Not much was known about this young king. However, his tomb was found completely intact, and this was remarkable. Most Egyptian tombs had been robbed of their treasures over the centuries. The rubble of other tombs had hidden the tomb of Tutankhamen. Grave robbers had not been able to locate his burial place. None of his artifacts had been stolen. Opened in 1922 by Howard Carter, it was a great find for archeology. This tomb in the Valley of the Kings gave us all kinds of information about ancient Egyptian culture that we had not known before.

When the tomb was opened, a stone sarcophagus was found inside of the innermost shrine. Inside the sarcophagus, there were three coffins nested inside one another. The innermost of these coffins was made of solid gold. This coffin held the mummy of King Tutankhamen. When it was opened, the mummified body of Tutankhamen was found. He was wearing a gold mask befitting his position as a king. The actual body of Tutankhamen had been preserved for all of these centuries.

The Egyptians had their own religion. They believed in life after death. They believed that

Integrating Ancient Civilizations with Reading Instruction © 2002 Creative Teaching Press

during the day the spirit would freely visit the afterworld. Then, at night, the spirit had to return to its body. Therefore, the body had to be in a form that was recognizable by the spirit. So the Egyptians practiced the art of mummification. They believed the spirit could recognize this preserved form. The mummy was then placed in a tomb.

Tombs were built by the Egyptians to hold the remains of the deceased. They wanted their leaders to have as good of a life in the afterworld as they did while on earth. Such things as household goods, weapons, cosmetics, games, and furniture were placed in the tomb as well. At first, these tombs were grand structures. These structures easily attracted the attention of grave robbers. Later, tombs were cut into the hillside at the Valley of the Kings. The Egyptians took great care to disguise the entrances. However, most of these tombs were found and robbed anyway. The Egyptians had practiced the process of mummification, or embalming, for thirty centuries. In addition to people, the Egyptians also embalmed animals. Many animals were revered by the Egyptians and were honored by being embalmed.

The process to make a mummy took as long as seventy days. After death, all internal organs were removed except for the heart, which was believed to hold a person's intelligence and emotions. The brain was removed through the nostrils in order to leave the skull intact. Next, the body was packed in natron, a salt, and left to dry for forty days. After the body was dried, it was stuffed with fragrant herbs and sawdust. Then, the outside was rubbed with oils and resins. The body was then wrapped in strips of linen as jewels and amulets were tucked into the wrappings. After this, the mummy was laid to rest in a coffin, or set of nested coffins, made of wood, clay, or stone.

With all of this elaborate preparation, the body was supposed to rest undisturbed for eternity. Most mummies did not. Their tombs were robbed for the riches buried there. The mummies themselves were not worthless. However, they were not treated with the reverence that the deceased are due. They were sold for a variety of purposes. Some people believed that if the mummy were ground up, the powder could be used to cure ailments. Sometimes the mummies were sold to wealthy Europeans who displayed them in their homes as a souvenir. Only one mummy and his tomb remained intact for over 3,000 years. The mummy of King Tutankhamen has survived to share its sercrets.

Integrating Ancient Civilizations with Reading Instruction © 2002 Creative Teaching Press

Comprehension Questions

Literal Questions

1. Who was King Tutankhamen? Why was he important?
2. What was the life span of Tutankhamen? What happened when he died?
3. Who is credited with the discovery of the tomb? Why was King Tut's tomb unharmed when it was discovered?
4. What was the mummification process?
5. What were the Egyptians' religious beliefs? Use details from the story to explain your answer.

Inferential Questions

1. Why do you think so many graves were robbed?
2. What do you think the scientific knowledge of the Egyptians was like at the time of King Tut's death? Use details from the story to explain your answer.
3. Do you think that everyone who died underwent the mummification process? Why or why not?
4. What tools and expertise do you think archeologists trying to excavate a tomb would need? When King Tut's sarcophagus was opened for the first time, what do you think the archeologists said?
5. Do you think it was respectful for people to buy the mummies and use them as souvenirs? Why or why not?

Making Connections

1. Look up *paleontology* in the dictionary or encyclopedia. How is archeology like paleontology? List at least three similarities and differences.
2. Do you think there are any other hidden mummies buried someplace in Egypt waiting to be discovered by archeologists? Why or why not?
3. In what ways does our society today emulate the Egyptian style?
4. If you could ask Howard Carter one question, what would it be? Why?
5. Do you think anyone is still practicing the art and science of mummification? Why or why not?

Sharpen Your Skills

1 How would you split the word "excavation" into syllables?

- ◯ ex-ca-vation
- ◯ ex-ca-va-tion
- ◯ exc-a-va-tion
- ◯ e-x-cava-tion

2 Which of the following sentences does not use the apostrophe correctly?

- ◯ Howard Carter's discovery was a tribute to archeology.
- ◯ According to all archeologists', it's amazing that the body was so well preserved.
- ◯ Most archeologists hope that King Tut's tomb wasn't the only one left intact.
- ◯ The touring exhibit of King Tut's treasures ended in 1979.

3 What part of speech is "the archeologist" in the following sentence?

Howard Carter, **the archeologist,** opened the tomb in the Valley of the Kings.

- ◯ conjunction
- ◯ interjection
- ◯ appositive
- ◯ noun of a direct address

4 What does the word "position" mean in the following sentence?

He was wearing a gold mask befitting his **position** as a king.

- ◯ loyalty
- ◯ idea
- ◯ status
- ◯ location

5 Which word would finish this analogy?

Burrito is to **tortilla** as **mummy** is to _____.

- ◯ tomb
- ◯ linens
- ◯ jewels
- ◯ oils and herbs

6 What kind of sentence is this?

The exhibit traveled across the United States.

- ◯ simple sentence
- ◯ complex sentence
- ◯ fragment
- ◯ run-on

7 Which words best complete the following sentence?

People saw many artifacts which _____ been damaged.

- ◯ has not
- ◯ had not
- ◯ are not
- ◯ did not

Integrating Ancient Civilizations with Reading Instruction © 2002 Creative Teaching Press

Get Logical

Melanie researched the excavation of and other important facts related to King Tut. Her report was comprised of five main sections. Use the clues below to decide what the topic was for each section of her report.

Clues

❶ Melanie began her report with a synopsis of King Tut's birth and youth.

❷ The final section did not discuss any artifacts.

❸ The discussion about the practice Egyptians had to help spirits recognize a preserved form of a body was exactly in the middle of her report.

❹ The section that discussed the items King Tut was buried with was after the section that discussed the location of many tombs.

❺ The reason tombs were cut into a hillside was discussed in a section prior to the location of the hillside.

	Section 1	Section 2	Section 3	Section 4	Section 5
Royal Artifacts					
The Boy King					
Valley of the Kings					
Grave Robbers					
Mummification					

The topic of section 1 was _____.

The topic of section 2 was _____.

The topic of section 3 was _____.

The topic of section 4 was _____.

The topic of section 5 was _____.

Bracelet fragment

Finger ring

Ear plugs

Egyptian Research

Purpose

The purpose of this activity is to help students piece together all of the various areas of interest that Egypt's history inspires. Students will complete a two-part project that includes an individual report and a group presentation.

MATERIALS

✔ Egyptian Research Guide (page 29)

✔ research materials related to Egypt's history (e.g., books, short stories, articles, films)

Implementation

Brainstorm with students a list of high-interest topics related to Egypt, and write them on the chalkboard. Some examples include pyramids, mummies, gods and goddesses, the Nile River, pharaohs, tombs, and King Tut. Divide the class into groups of two to three students. Assign one topic to each group. (If you have a larger class size, assign some topics to more than one group.) Provide research materials, and give each student an Egyptian Research Guide. Have students use these materials to begin their research in class. Encourage them to research their topic outside of class as well. Have each student write a two-page report based on his or her research. Invite students to create a cover and draw illustrations to accompany their report. Then, ask each group of students to create a presentation. Give students at least one week to create and organize it. Review with students the group presentation requirements outlined on the Egyptian Research Guide. Invite each group to share their presentation with the rest of the class.

Integrating Ancient Civilizations with Reading Instruction © 2002 Creative Teaching Press

Name _____ Date _____

Egyptian Research Guide

Topic:

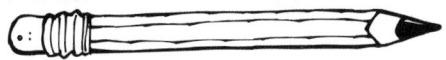 **Written Report**

Write a two-page report giving an overview of the information for your research topic.
Answer these questions in your report:

1 How were Egyptians' lives affected by your topic?

2 In what ways was your topic practiced during Egypt's history?

3 Is your area of research still important to Egyptians today? In what ways?

4 Explain three new and interesting facts you learned about your topic.

5 What more would you like to know about your research topic?

6 Create a cover and draw illustrations to accompany your report.

 **Group Presentation Requirements**

Organize a group presentation that provides a clear understanding of your area of research.
Use the following guidelines for your presentation:

1 Split your presentation evenly so that every group member has a speaking part.

2 Create a list of important facts about your topic. Present them in a creative way.

3 Use at least one type of technology or media in your presentation. Some examples
include an overhead projector, film, slides, music, or posters.

4 The presentation should last at least 5 minutes but no more than 20 minutes.

5 Have fun showcasing your area of expertise!

Catch a Clue

What will we learn about in our reading today?

Pyramids of Egypt

Lighthouse of Alexandria

Seven Wonders of the Ancient World

Hanging Gardens of Babylon

Great Wall of China

1 We will read about a popular tourist attraction.

2 It was built over 2,000 years ago.

3 We will not learn about a structure located in Africa.

4 We will learn about a landmark that was used to protect people and transport troops.

Integrating Ancient Civilizations with Reading Instruction © 2002 Creative Teaching Press

Concept Map

Facts we already know about the **Great Wall of China**, and the new facts we have learned

The Great Wall of China

Word Warm-Up

Which words might you expect to find in a story about the **Great Wall of China?**

conquered	barrier	immense
emperor	prosperity	revolt
porcelain	continuous	structure
erected	rocket	reign

Integrating Ancient Civilizations with Reading Instruction © 2002 Creative Teaching Press

The Great Wall of China

China is a country on the continent of Asia. It is the third largest country in the world. It has the world's largest number of people. China also has the world's oldest living civilization. While other civilizations are older, China is the only one that is still in existence today. The written history of China goes back about 3,500 years. The Chinese take great pride in their long history. They are proud of the influence that their country has had on other nations. Inventors in China were the first to produce the compass, porcelain, paper, and silk cloth. China has made many contributions to the world.

Every year many tourists visit China to experience the land and the culture. The most popular tourist attraction there is the Great Wall of China. Many people visit China with the intention of walking the Great Wall.

The Great Wall of China is an ancient structure. It has survived over 2,000 years. Before 221 B.C., the wall was made up of a series of short walls made of rammed earth. During the Qin Dynasty, these shorter walls were joined together into one Great Wall. Stone and brick were used to reinforce the wall. Today, the Great Wall itself is more than 3,700 miles (5,955 km) long, although the distance it covers is even greater. This is because the wall is not continuous. Parts of it have crumbled or been destroyed. These missing sections had not been replaced over the years.

The Great Wall stands at about 30 feet (9 m) high. Forty-foot (12.2-m) towers stand at every 100 to 200 yards (91 to 183 m) along the wall. These towers served as lookout posts. The Great Wall is 25 feet (7.6 m) wide at its base and narrows to 15 feet (4.5 m) in width at the top. The top of the wall served as a road for the movement of troops and horses. It is wide enough for three horsemen to ride side-by-side.

Emperor Shi-Huangdi of the Qin Dynasty was the ruler who first began a planned building of the Great Wall. He was an emperor, or ruler, who favored *big* construction projects. His empire was one of peace and stability. He kept a huge military, but they did not have much fighting to do. These large projects were a way for him to keep his soldiers busy and employed since they were not fighting other armies. In all, his big projects kept three million people employed. About 500,000 people worked on the Great Wall during this time. These workers spent between seven and ten years constructing the Great Wall.

Why did the emperor consider this immense project? The empire of China was fairly new. Originally, there were many small states within China that made their own rules. The Qin Dynasty was the first to bring all of these little states together into one empire. Emperor Shi-Huangdi wanted to protect his people from invaders and the uncivilized. He planned the Great Wall as a barrier to keep out enemies. However, he also built the wall with the idea of keeping his own citizens from leaving. The Great Wall may have been built for protection, but it did not always work. If the attacks were minor, then it did keep out the invaders. If the attack was a major one, the Great Wall was ineffective at stopping it. In the 1200s, Genghis Khan of the Mongols swept over the wall and conquered China.

In the mid 1300s, a peasant named Hong Wu led a revolt that expelled the Mongols from China. Hong Wu became the new emperor. The Ming Dynasty had begun. Hong Wu was able to restore China's national pride. His reign was a time of good government, peace, and prosperity. He abolished slavery and redistributed some of the wealth of the rich to the poor. Chinese arts and culture flourished during this time.

The Ming Dynasty was responsible for repairing or rebuilding much of the Great Wall. They also lengthened the wall. The Great Wall of China we see today is a result of their efforts. At the time of the Ming Dynasty, much of the wall was in disrepair. It had not been maintained properly and was falling apart. The restoration of the wall by the Ming Dynasty lasted for 200 years. Their main intent was to rebuild and reinforce the wall to keep out invaders.

Today, the Great Wall of China is an awe-inspiring sight. It is the largest structure ever built by man. Although it is not actually visible from outer space, it is visible from a plane. The Great Wall is still releasing its secrets to us. Historians study artifacts and tombs uncovered along the structure to learn about China's civilization long ago. The Great Wall of China will continue to be an attraction for years, maybe centuries, to come.

Integrating Ancient Civilizations with Reading Instruction © 2002 Creative Teaching Press

Comprehension Questions

Literal Questions

1. What is the main attraction people travel to China to visit? How long has it been in existence?
2. What is the succession of dynasties in China, beginning with the building of the Great Wall of China?
3. What was the original purpose of the Great Wall? How has that purpose changed over time?
4. What are the dimensions of the wall?
5. Why do historians still study the Great Wall after all these years?

Inferential Questions

1. Why do you think people are interested in visiting the Great Wall?
2. Why do you think that some dynasties took care of the wall and others did not?
3. Do you think the Great Wall will ever be completely restored to its original form? Why or why not?
4. What information about ancient China do you think could be hidden within or around the Great Wall?
5. Do you think the Great Wall helped China's citizens to feel safe? Why or why not?

Making Connections

1. Would you be interested in seeing the Great Wall in person someday? Why or why not?
2. Research the materials that were used in the construction of the Great Wall. What do you think life would have been like if you were one of the workers?
3. There was once talk of destroying the Great Wall. Why do you think people considered this? Would you support this action or oppose it? Why?
4. In your opinion, is the Great Wall worthy of being one of the greatest relics of the ancient world? Why or why not?
5. The Great Wall helped employ many people during a time when it might have been difficult to find work. Franklin D. Roosevelt did something similar to help end the Great Depression. Research three great building projects produced by the Works Project Administration that were part of Roosevelt's New Deal policy.

Name _____   Date _____

Sharpen Your Skills

① What is the best synonym for the word "served" in the following sentence?

The top of the wall **served** as a road for the movement of troops and horses.

- ○ dished up
- ○ acted
- ○ gave out
- ○ completed

② Which sentence uses correct subject-verb agreement?

- ○ The Great Wall of China represent a lasting culture.
- ○ The Great Wall of China represents a lasting culture.
- ○ The Great Wall of China representing a lasting culture.
- ○ The Great Wall of China representative of a lasting culture.

③ What part of speech is the word "that" in the following sentence?

Do you want to borrow **that** book on China?

- ○ adverb
- ○ modifier
- ○ interjection
- ○ conjunction

④ What does the word "originally" mean in the following sentence?

Originally, there were many small states within China that made their own rules.

- ○ to conclude
- ○ lastly
- ○ moderately
- ○ initially

⑤ Which words would finish this analogy?

Build is to _____ as **rebuild** is to _____.

- ○ Mongols/Hong Wu
- ○ Hong Wu/Mongols
- ○ Ming Dynasty/Qin Dynasty
- ○ Qin Dynasty/Ming Dynasty

⑥ What kind of sentence is the following sentence?

And the Great Wall of China.

- ○ simple sentence
- ○ fragment
- ○ complex sentence
- ○ run-on

⑦ Which words would best complete the following sentence?

Some of the wall _____ to the ground.

- ○ did fallen
- ○ had fell
- ○ did fell
- ○ had fallen

Integrating Ancient Civilizations with Reading Instruction © 2002 Creative Teaching Press

Get Logical

The television show Jeopardy had a category titled "China." The clues were worth $100 to $500 increasing in order of difficulty. The answers are listed below. Use the clues below to decide which statement was worth each amount of money.

Clues

❶ The question worth the most money did not deal with a person or people.

❷ The $200 question stated, "What three products were the Chinese the first to make?"

❸ "Who was responsible for rebuilding the Great Wall?" This question was worth less than $300.

❹ The $400 question was not "Who are the Qins?"

	$100	$200	$300	$400	$500
The Dynasty That Built the Great Wall					
More Than 3,700 Miles					
Porcelain, Paper, Silk					
Ming Dynasty					
Mongols					

The answer to the $100 question was _____.

The answer to the $200 question was _____.

The answer to the $300 question was _____.

The answer to the $400 question was _____.

The answer to the $500 question was _____.

Integrating Ancient Civilizations with Reading Instruction © 2002 Creative Teaching Press

Great Wall of Facts: China

Purpose

The purpose of this activity is for students to showcase all of the important facts they gained in studying China. In addition, students will use their facts to build a "Great Wall" of Chinese culture facts to display in the classroom.

MATERIALS

✔ Great Brick Wall reproducible (page 39)
✔ red construction paper
✔ research materials (e.g, books, story on pages 33–34, encyclopedias)
✔ scissors

Implementation

Explain to students that the Great Wall of China was created and maintained over several centuries and is one of the biggest tourist attractions in China today. Copy a class set of the Great Brick Wall reproducible on red construction paper. Have students use research materials to find facts about Chinese culture. Ask them to record at least 14 facts and then check their work for any spelling errors. Give each student a Great Brick Wall reproducible. Ask students to write each of their facts inside a "brick" on their paper. Have them cut out their wall. Use the cutouts to create a "Great Wall" of Chinese facts on a bulletin board, and add examples of Chinese art, poetry, writing, or maps to the display. Or, use the cutouts as the border for a bulletin board on China.

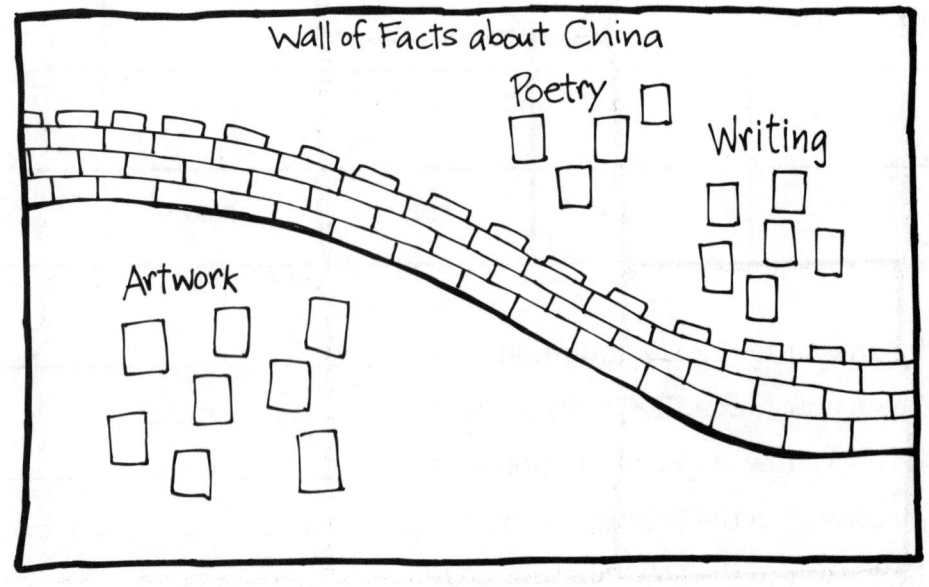

Integrating Ancient Civilizations with Reading Instruction © 2002 Creative Teaching Press

Great Brick Wall

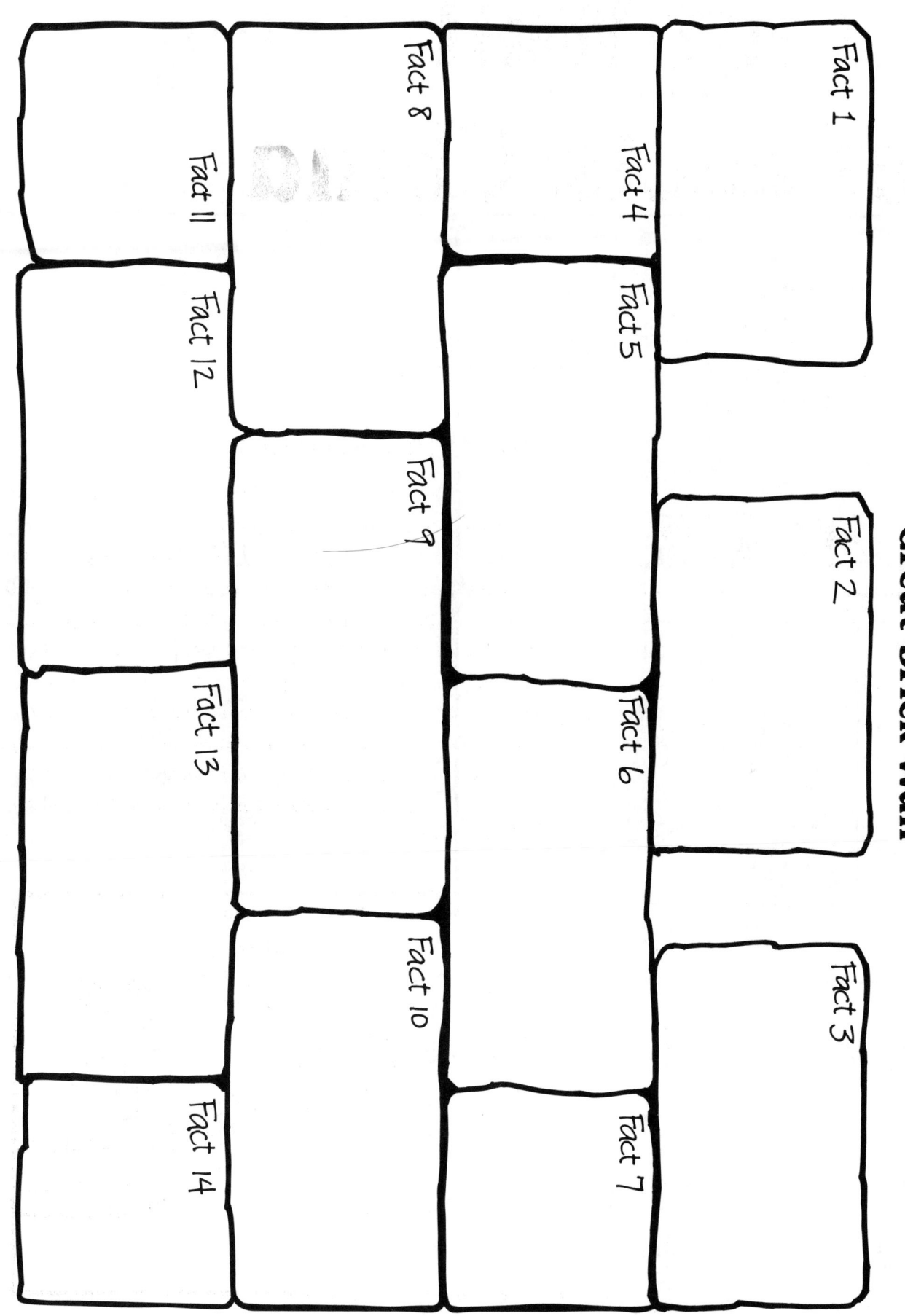

Fact 1

Fact 4

Fact 8

Fact 11

Fact 5

Fact 12

Fact 2

Fact 9

Fact 6

Fact 13

Fact 3

Fact 10

Fact 7

Fact 14

Catch a Clue

Aztecs

Olmecs

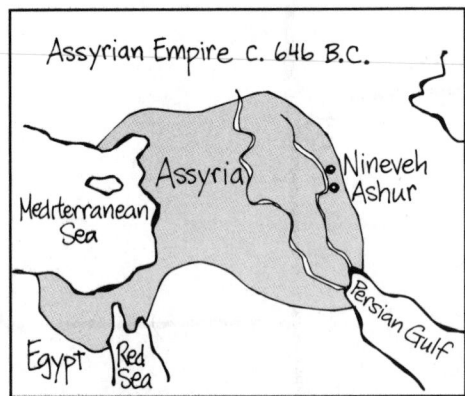

Assyrians

Homer
Greeks

1 We will not read about an ancient European civilization.

2 We will not focus our attention on an ancient civilization of Mesopotamia.

3 We will focus on South America.

4 We will learn about a culture that began in 1500 B.C. and lasted until 400 B.C.

Integrating Ancient Civilizations with Reading Instruction © 2002 Creative Teaching Press

Concept Map

Facts we already know about the **Olmec civilization,** and the new facts we have learned

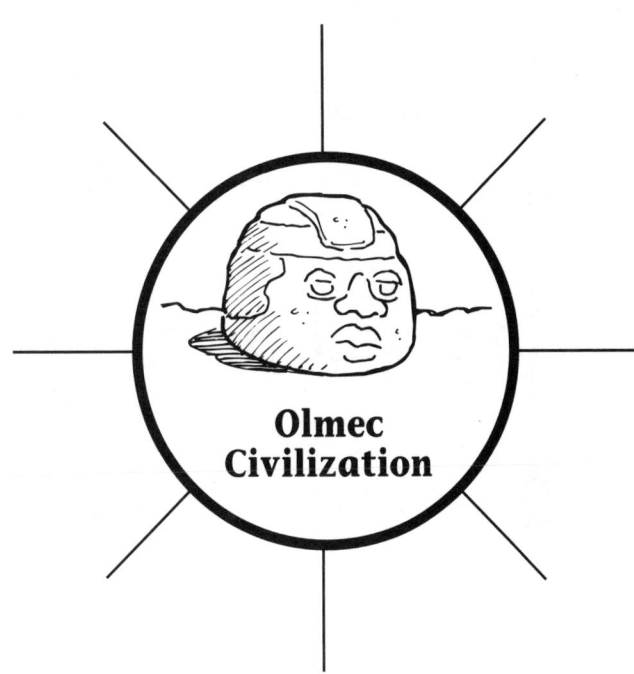

Olmec Civilization

Word Warm-Up

Olmec Colossal Head in LaVenta Park, Villahermosa, Mexico

Which words might you expect to find in a story about the **Olmec civilization?**

naturalistic	arithmetic	hierarchy
technology	aqueducts	archeological
artifacts	mysteries	supernatural
deceased	pyramid	elaborate

Integrating Ancient Civilizations with Reading Instruction © 2002 Creative Teaching Press

Mystery of the Olmec

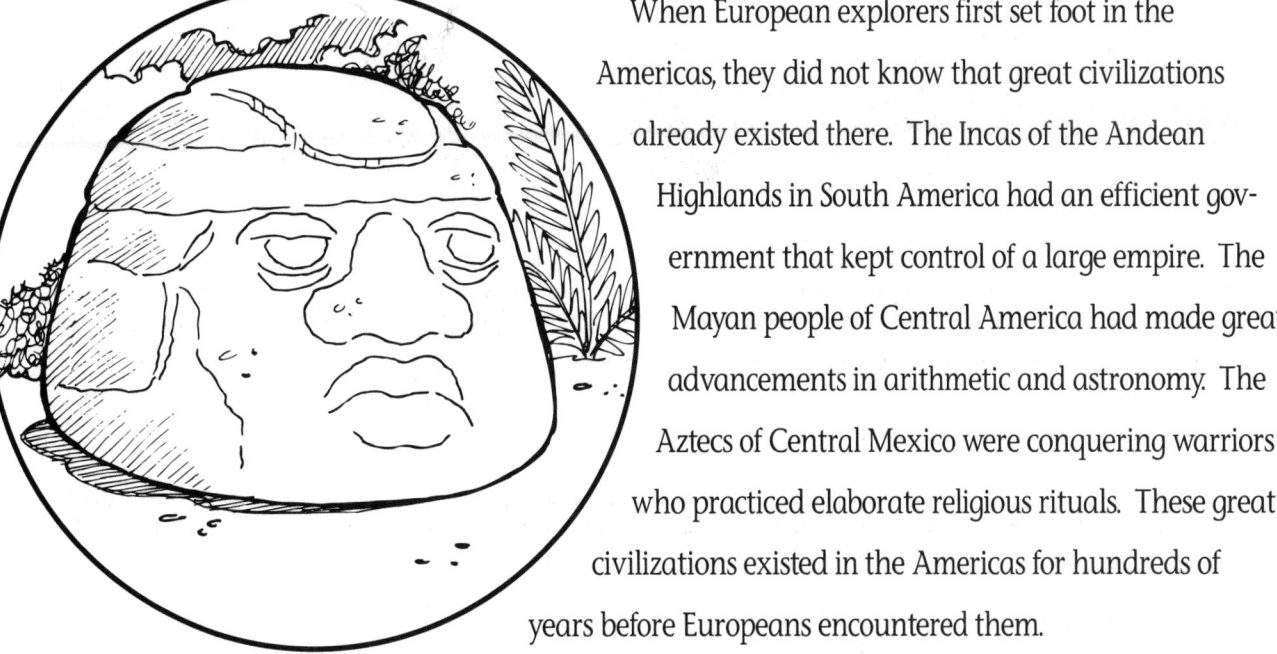

When European explorers first set foot in the Americas, they did not know that great civilizations already existed there. The Incas of the Andean Highlands in South America had an efficient government that kept control of a large empire. The Mayan people of Central America had made great advancements in arithmetic and astronomy. The Aztecs of Central Mexico were conquering warriors who practiced elaborate religious rituals. These great civilizations existed in the Americas for hundreds of years before Europeans encountered them.

The Aztecs, Incas, and Mayas were not the first civilizations to arise in the Americas. All three were preceded by the Olmec civilization. The Olmecs are considered the first true civilization of the New World.

When archeologists began to explore the region of Mexico, they discovered enormous stone heads. Each head was carved from a solid piece of basalt rock. Each head stood 8 to 12 feet (2.4 to 3.7 m) high and weighed as much as 36,000 pounds (16,344 kg). At first, scientists did not know who had carved these heads or what they meant. The heads were different than the artifacts of the Inca, Aztec, or Mayan people. Scientists were also baffled by the fact that each head had to be moved a great distance. The nearest basalt source was over 50 miles (80 km) away.

Much of what we now know about the Olmecs comes from studying their art. Through other archeological finds, scientists have learned that the Olmec people created these impressive heads. However, because they had no written record of their history, many mysteries remain about this ancient culture.

The Olmecs first appeared on the coast of the Gulf of Mexico. Their culture became established around 1500 B.C. and lasted until 400 B.C. The locations of La Venta, San Lorenzo, and Tres Zapotes are important sites of ancient Olmec civilizations. Scientists think that each site was the center of trade and religion for the region. Each site had a huge earthen pyramid that was up to 100 feet (30.5 m) in height. The pyramid consisted of a series of platforms. At the base of the pyramid, there were carvings of supernatural beings and important events. One of the sites also had what seems to be a ball court. Scientists do not know if this was for sports or served a religious purpose. They have found carved figures of athletes and wrestlers, so it appears that athletics were important to the Olmec culture.

The Olmecs had very little tool technology. Most of their tools were simple and changed little over time. For example, while the wheel appears on toys and models, the Olmecs never used the wheel to transport goods or people. They preferred to carry things on their backs. The Olmecs did make great achievements in art, science, and architecture. In addition to the carved heads, the Olmecs made naturalistic images of people and animals out of stone. They also carved jade and worked with gold, silver, and copper. They excelled in sculpture, molded clay figurines, and made pottery.

From their art we also know that the Olmecs practiced body painting and tattooing. We know that they filed their teeth as a sign of beauty. Both men and women shaved all or part of their heads. The Olmecs also altered the appearance of their infants to enhance their children's beauty. They would make the infant's skull longer by wrapping and pressing it while it was still soft. Crossed eyes were also considered attractive. The Olmecs would dangle a bead between a baby's eyes to train the eyes to cross.

The Olmec people are now believed to be a culture of many firsts for the Americas. They built the first pyramids and cities. They were the first society that had a hierarchy based on wealth and status. They designed the first aqueducts and a system of irrigation. The Olmecs developed a working calendar. They invented a language system of complex symbols. Many of these achievements were adopted later in the cultures of the Mayan, Inca, and Aztec peoples.

What eventually happened to the Olmec culture remains a mystery. The Olmec civilization disappeared around 400 B.C. There is no explanation or evidence as to why this happened. However, archeologists continue to look for evidence to explain the existence of this amazing ancient civilization.

Integrating Ancient Civilizations with Reading Instruction © 2002 Creative Teaching Press

Comprehension Questions

Literal Questions

❶ By what year did the Olmec civilization become established? About what year did it disappear?

❷ Describe the pyramids of the Olmec.

❸ How did the Olmecs alter the appearance of their infants? Why did they do this?

❹ How did the Olmecs alter their own appearance to make themselves more beautiful?

❺ Name at least three things that the Olmecs were the first to create.

Inferential Questions

❶ How do we know about the Olmec civilization today? What is still unknown about their culture? Why don't we know more about their culture?

❷ Why do you think the Olmecs knew about the wheel but did not use it to make transporting goods easier?

❸ How do you think the basalt rocks ended up as far as 50 miles (80 km) away from where they were originally found?

❹ What do you think a typical day in the Olmec civilization would be like? What would it include?

❺ What do you think the physical geography and climate were like for the Olmecs? Explain your answer.

Making Connections

❶ What are your opinions of the Olmecs' view of beauty? Discuss at least two different things they did and how you feel about them.

❷ If you could travel back in time to spend one week with the Olmecs, what would you want to see the most? What would you want to do? Why?

❸ Research what else has been discovered about this ancient civilization, who first discovered the relics, and what life was like for children in their culture.

❹ If you wanted to explore the ancient Olmec civilization, where would you go? Look at a map to determine the best way to get there.

❺ Do you use or benefit from anything today that the Olmecs created? If so, what do you use or benefit from?

Sharpen Your Skills

1 What is the best synonym for the word "altered" in this sentence?

The Olmecs also **altered** the appearance of their infants.

- ○ maintained
- ○ destroyed
- ○ marred
- ○ changed

2 Which of the following sentences does <u>not</u> use the comma correctly?

- ○ The Aztecs, Incas, and Mayas were not the first civilizations in America.
- ○ There were carvings of supernatural beings, and important events.
- ○ At first, scientists did not know who had carved these heads or what they meant.
- ○ However, archeologists continue to look for evidence to explain the existence of this amazing ancient civilization.

3 What part of speech is the word "so" in the following sentence?

Carved figures of athletes and wrestlers have been found, **so** it appears that athletics were important to the Olmec culture.

- ○ superlative adjective
- ○ interjection
- ○ appositive
- ○ conjunction

4 What does the word "impressive" mean in the following sentence?

Scientists have learned that the Olmec people created these **impressive** heads.

- ○ recreational
- ○ ordinary
- ○ remarkable
- ○ disgusting

5 Which words would finish this analogy?

Olmecs are to _____ as **Syrians** are to _____.

- ○ ancient/current
- ○ Mesopotamia/Gulf of Mexico
- ○ men/women
- ○ Gulf of Mexico/Mesopotamia

6 What kind of sentence is the following sentence?

They carved basalt rock.

- ○ simple sentence
- ○ complex sentence
- ○ fragment
- ○ run-on

7 Which word or phrase best completes the following sentence?

Many aspects of the Olmec civilization _____ unknown to this day.

- ○ remains
- ○ is remaining
- ○ remained
- ○ remain

Integrating Ancient Civilizations with Reading Instruction © 2002 Creative Teaching Press

Name _____   Date _____

Get Logical

Gino researched the Olmec civilization and learned many interesting facts. His report was comprised of five main sections. Use the clues below to decide what the topic was for each section of his report.

Clues

❶ The section that discussed how the Olmecs created cross-eyed children is an even number.
❷ Gino began his report by discussing where people could go to see the carvings.
❸ The final section did not discuss advancements or inventions, nor did it discuss mysteries for scientists today.
❹ The fact that the Olmecs created an irrigation system is mentioned in the third section of Gino's report.
❺ The section that discussed scientific mysteries that remain today came before the section about the Olmecs' view of beauty.

	Section 1	Section 2	Section 3	Section 4	Section 5
Location					
Mysteries to This Day					
Beautification					
Inventions/ Advancements					
An Artistic Culture					

The topic of section 1 was _____.

The topic of section 2 was _____.

The topic of section 3 was _____.

The topic of section 4 was _____.

The topic of section 5 was _____.

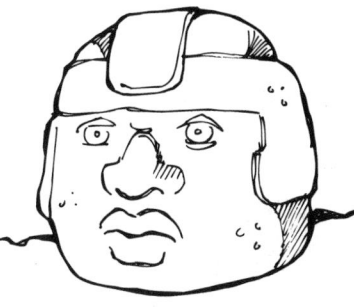

Integrating Ancient Civilizations with Reading Instruction © 2002 Creative Teaching Press

Olmec Art

Purpose

The purpose of this activity is to let students express themselves through art, specifically carving. Students will carve their own head in a piece of soft soap or clay.

MATERIALS

- ✔ paper to cover work area
- ✔ bars of soft soap or pieces of clay
- ✔ plastic forks, knives, and spoons
- ✔ toothpicks
- ✔ index cards

Implementation

Explain to students that much of what we know about the Olmecs comes from studying their artwork. Most of their art was in the form of carvings. The basalt heads that the Olmecs carved were often over 8 feet (2.4 m) high and weighed over 36,000 pounds (16,344 kg). The exact purpose of the heads is still a mystery. Discuss with students why a group of people might carve such large pieces of art. List the students' ideas on the chalkboard. Then, explain to students that art is a way for a group of people to leave behind evidence of their existence. This evidence is often looked at by later groups of people and interpreted. Sometimes the interpretations are correct and sometimes they are wrong. Explain that, in any case, art is an expression of who a group is and what is important to them. Tell students that they will be expressing themselves through art. Explain that they are going to carve a representation of their own head. Have students cover their desks with paper. Give each student a bar of soft soap or a piece of clay. Invite students to use a plastic knife to carve the shape of their head. Once students have carved the basic shape, have them use a plastic fork, spoon, and/or toothpick to carve additional details on their soap or clay head. Tell students it is important to carve small areas at a time and not to rush. Give students an index card. Have them write their name on it and place it under their carved head. Display the final products together as the Olmec heads were often displayed.

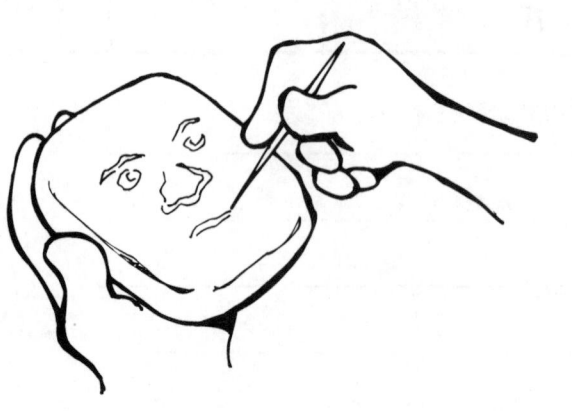

Integrating Ancient Civilizations with Reading Instruction © 2002 Creative Teaching Press

Catch a Clue

What will we learn about in our reading today?

ancient emperors

Homer

Greek mythology

Roman gods

Engravings on a stone slab

the Sumerians

1 We will **read** about those who were honored.

2 We will **not** focus our attention on people who are no longer alive.

3 We will learn more about an ancient religion.

4 Our learning will **not** involve Italy.

Concept Map

Facts we already know about **Greek gods and goddesses,** and the new facts we have learned

**Greek Gods
and Goddesses**

Integrating Ancient Civilizations with Reading Instruction © 2002 Creative Teaching Press

Word Warm-Up

Athena   Dionysus

Which words might you expect to find in a story about **Greek gods and goddesses?**

superhuman	deities	scripture
ceremonies	characters	polytheistic
disguise	valleys	philosophers
oracle	vegetation	storyteller

Greek Gods and Goddesses

Greece is a country whose recorded history goes back to 3000 B.C. The ancient Greeks made great achievements in government, philosophy, science, and the arts. These achievements influence our civilizations today.

Greece developed as small city-states. A city-state was made up of a city or town and the villages and farmland that surrounded it. Each city-state was very independent. These various communities were never united into one nation. However, they did share a common language, culture, and religion.

The religion of the ancient Greeks was created to explain the world around them. The ancient Greeks were polytheistic. This means that they worshipped many deities. A deity is a god or a goddess. There was no written scripture, so the qualities and actions of these deities could change with the storyteller.

The people believed that these gods and goddesses watched over them and had an influence over their daily activities. Each household would try to please their chosen deity with offerings and ceremonies. Each city-state also honored one or more of these deities. They were considered protectors of the community. People built temples and held annual festivals in their honor.

The gods and goddesses of ancient Greece were mainly represented in human form. Unlike humans, they were immortal and had superhuman powers. They also had the ability to disguise themselves as other humans or animals on earth. Some represented good and some evil. Their behavior showed love, hate, jealousy, and anger.

The gods and goddesses of ancient Greece formed a family. These deities made their home on Mount Olympus. From here, they were able to attend to their own affairs, as well as watch over the affairs of mortals on Earth. Twelve main deities lived on Mount Olympus: Zeus, Hera, Athena, Ares, Apollo,

Integrating Ancient Civilizations with Reading Instruction © 2002 Creative Teaching Press

Artemis, Hermes, Dionysus, Poseidon, Aphrodite, Demeter, and Hephaestus. Hades was another main god, but he did not live on Mount Olympus.

Zeus was considered the king of the gods. He ruled over Mount Olympus. He was the lord of the skies. Hera was the wife of Zeus. She was the goddess of marriage and protector of childbirth.

Zeus was also father to many other deities. Athena was a daughter of Zeus and was born from his head. She was the goddess of war. Athena was also the protector of those skills women used in their homes. She protected weaving, needlework, sewing, and other domestic crafts. She was an advisory of Ares, a son of Zeus's. Ares was the god of war. Apollo and Artemis were twin children of Zeus. Apollo was the god of oracles. An oracle was a place where one's future could be revealed. He was also the protector of music. He could bring sickness or health to an individual. Artemis was the goddess of all wild animals. She was the protector of nature and hunting. Hermes was another son of Zeus. He served as the messenger of the gods. Hermes was the protector of shepherds, heralds, and thieves. His job was also to help guide the souls of the dead to the underworld. Dionysus was another son of Zeus and the god of wine.

Poseidon was Zeus's brother. He was the lord of the waters, earthquakes, and horses. Together with Zeus, they both watched over earth. Hades was another brother of Zeus. He was the god of the dead and ruler of the underworld.

Aphrodite was the goddess of love and all things romantic. She was the daughter of no one. She was born out of the sea. Demeter was the goddess of agriculture and had influence over the seasons. Hephaestus was the god of fire and protector of blacksmiths.

In addition, there were other minor gods and goddesses. There were also half-mortals and heroic mortals who were favored by the gods. All of these characters played parts in stories that helped explain the workings of nature and mankind. Over time, the views of the Greek people began to change. As humans began to better understand nature and science, they began to believe less in the deities. Philosophers started to question the influence of the gods. They even began to explore new belief systems where there was one god who was more important than the others. They also considered the idea that there was only one god and no others. Some even wondered if there were any gods or goddesses at all. These new ideas meant an end to the belief in the gods and goddesses of Mount Olympus.

Comprehension Questions

Literal Questions

❶ In which four areas did the Greeks make great achievements?

❷ What was a city-state? What were some characteristics of a city-state?

❸ Who were the god and goddess of war? How were they related? Who was their father?

❹ Name the twelve main deities that resided on Mount Olympus in alphabetical order.

❺ What form were the Greek gods and goddesses mainly represented in? How could they disguise themselves? What emotions did their behavior show?

Inferential Questions

❶ You read about polytheism. What would you assume monotheism means? Do you know what groups of people believe in it?

❷ Create a family tree beginning with Zeus. Include all of the gods and goddesses mentioned in this story.

❸ How did we learn about Greek gods and goddesses if the information was not written down?

❹ Why do you think each household would try to please their chosen deity?

❺ Because there was no written scripture, qualities and actions about deities could change with each new storyteller. Explain why this is probably true.

Making Connections

❶ If you had to choose one Greek god or goddess to research further, which would you choose? Why?

❷ Rank the gods and goddesses in order from one (being your favorite) to twelve (being your least favorite). Explain why your favorite and least favorite are in those positions.

❸ Draw a picture of what you think your favorite god or goddess looked like.

❹ Research where the names for the gods and goddesses come from.

❺ Why do you think people in our society today are so fascinated with the Greek gods and goddesses?

Integrating Ancient Civilizations with Reading Instruction © 2002 Creative Teaching Press

Sharpen Your Skills

Name _____   Date _____

1 What is the best synonym for the word "operations" in the following sentence?

The citizens were involved in the **operations** and concerns of their city-state.

- ○ surgeries
- ○ positions
- ○ mechanics
- ○ workings

2 If you wanted to find out more about a god or goddess, which resource would be the most helpful?

- ○ thesaurus
- ○ dictionary
- ○ encyclopedia
- ○ almanac

3 Look at these names: Athena—Ares—Aphrodite—Dionysus.

Which name does <u>not</u> belong with the others?

- ○ Athena
- ○ Aphrodite
- ○ Ares
- ○ Dionysus

4 In which sentence is the word "please" used in the same way as in the following sentence?

Each household would try to **please** their chosen deity with offerings and ceremonies.

- ○ Would you please help me?
- ○ May I please read one more chapter?
- ○ It would please me if your report included a complete bibliography.
- ○ She never even said, "Please!"

5 Which words would finish this analogy?

Athena is to _____ as **Aphrodite** is to _____.

- ○ love/ocean
- ○ fire/sky
- ○ war/love
- ○ needlework/agriculture

6 How would you split the word "polytheistic" into syllables?

- ○ poly-theis-tic
- ○ pol-ytheis-tic
- ○ po-ly-the-is-tic
- ○ po-ly-thei-stic

7 Which word or phrase best completes the following sentence?

Polytheism _____ to come to an end when monotheism started to gain in popularity.

- ○ began
- ○ have begun
- ○ begins
- ○ begun again

Integrating Ancient Civilizations with Reading Instruction © 2002 Creative Teaching Press

Name _____   Date _____

 Get Logical

Conner, Ferdos, Solon, Tanner, and Sydney are students in Ms. Hamada's Writer's Workshop. They have published books on gods and goddesses of Greek mythology. Use the clues below to decide which god or goddess each student wrote about.

Clues

❶ Solon's report did not focus on a goddess.

❷ The book written about the goddess of agriculture was not authored by Connor or Ferdos.

❸ The book that discussed the god people would honor if they were going out in the sea was not written by Solon, Tanner, or Sydney.

❹ Sydney's book featured the goddess of love and all things romantic.

❺ Connor's book was written about a goddess and featured a husband and wife.

	Conner	Ferdos	Solon	Tanner	Sydney
Aphrodite					
Hera					
Poseidon					
Demeter					
Hephaestus					

Connor's published book features _____.

Ferdos's published book features _____.

Solon's published book features _____.

Tanner's published book features _____.

Sydney's published book features _____.

Integrating Ancient Civilizations with Reading Instruction © 2002 Creative Teaching Press

Greek Game

Purpose

The purpose of this activity is to give students a chance to better understand each Greek god and goddess and the area he or she ruled over. Students will play a card game that will reinforce their knowledge of the gods and goddesses.

MATERIALS

- ✔ Gods and Goddesses Playing Cards (pages 58–61)
- ✔ Greek Game Scoring Guide (page 62)
- ✔ tagboard, card stock, or construction paper
- ✔ scissors
- ✔ lined or blank paper

Implementation

Explain to students that the Greeks were a polytheistic society, meaning they believed in many gods. These gods and goddesses controlled the many aspects of the Greeks' lives, which they did not feel they had control over. Each god or goddess had a particular area of responsibility. Copy on tagboard, card stock, or construction paper a set of the Gods and Goddesses Playing Cards for each group of two to three students. Cut apart the cards. Explain the rules of the game and the scoring guide. Post the Greek Game Scoring Guide for students to easily score each hand they have and to determine the overall winner.

Rules

1. The dealer deals five cards to each player and places the rest of the cards facedown in a pile.
2. Moving from one player to another, the dealer asks players if they would like to exchange any cards.
3. Each player may discard up to three cards and draw new ones from the top of the deck.
4. After the card exchange is complete, the players place their cards faceup on the table.
5. The players use the scoring guide to calculate their score and record it on a piece of paper.
6. The dealer collects all the cards and shuffles them for the next hand.
7. Have students continue playing the game until you call time.
8. Ask players to total their points. The player with the most points wins the game.

Gods and Goddesses Playing Cards

King of the Gods and Lord of the Skies	Lord of the Water
Goddess of Marriage and Childbirth	Goddess of Wild Animals
Messenger of the Gods	God of Fire

Integrating Ancient Civilizations with Reading Instruction © 2002 Creative Teaching Press

Gods and Goddesses Playing Cards

Goddess of War and Protector of Women's Skills	God of War
God of the Oracles and Protector of Music	Goddess of Agriculture
God of Wine	Goddess of Love

Gods and Goddesses Playing Cards

Zeus

Hera

Poseidon

Athena

Apollo

Artemis

Gods and Goddesses Playing Cards

Aphrodite

Hermes

Demeter

Dionysus

Hephaestus

Ares

Greek Game Scoring Guide

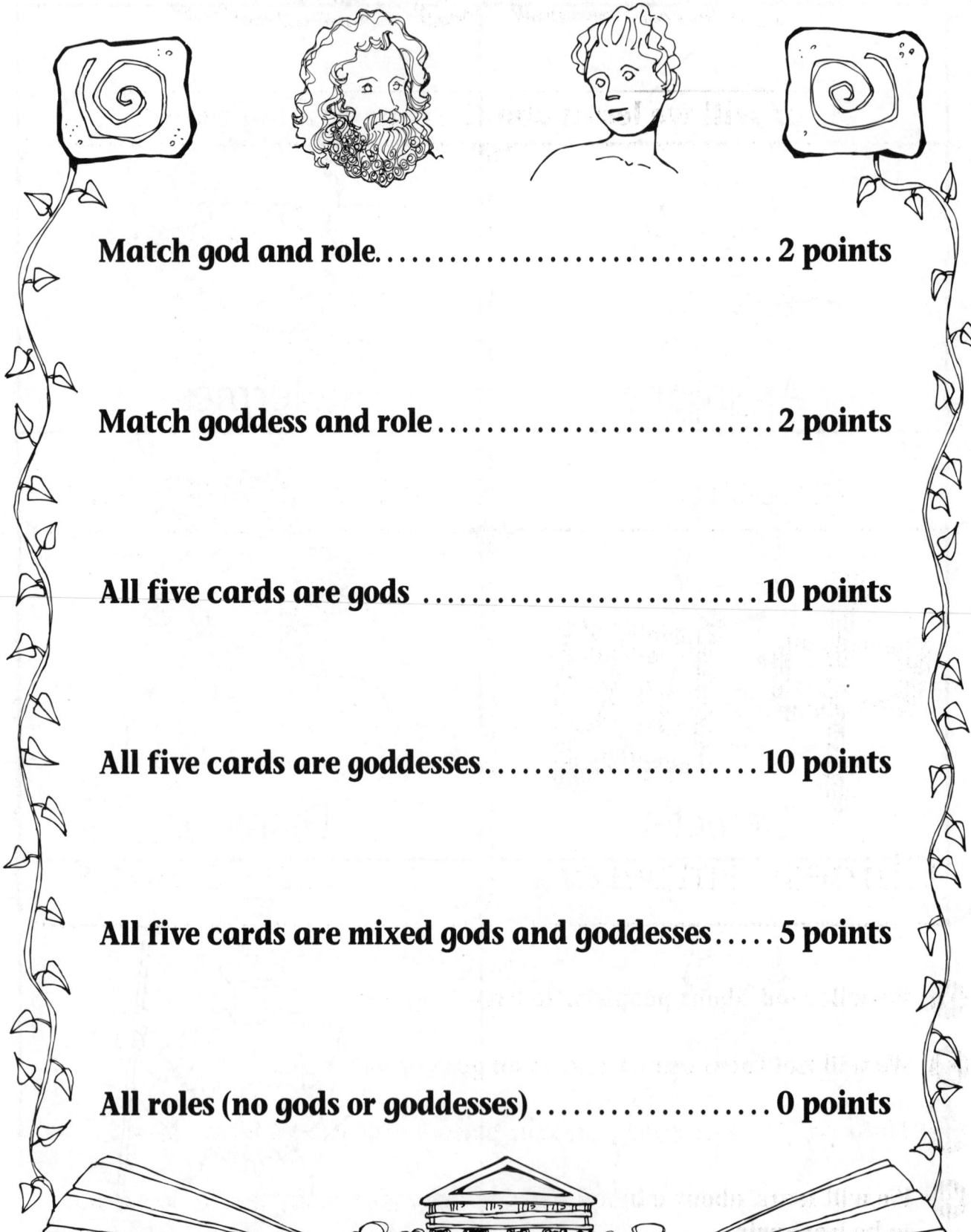

Match god and role . . . . 2 points

Match goddess and role . . . . 2 points

All five cards are gods . . . . 10 points

All five cards are goddesses . . . . 10 points

All five cards are mixed gods and goddesses . . . . . 5 points

All roles (no gods or goddesses) . . . . 0 points

Integrating Ancient Civilizations with Reading Instruction © 2002 Creative Teaching Press

Catch a Clue

What will we learn about in our reading today?

gladiators

Greek mythology

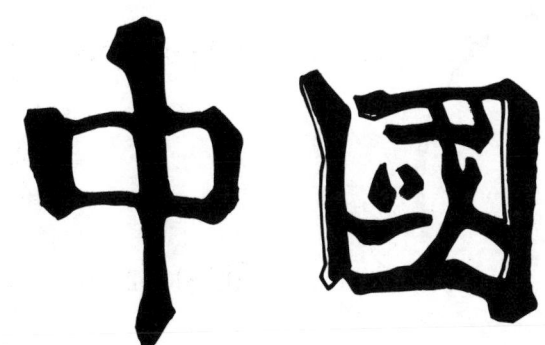

Chinese emperors

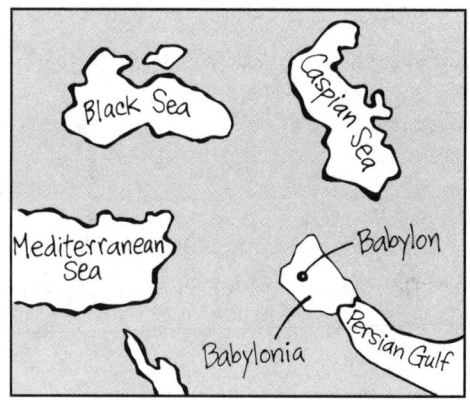

the Babylonians

1 We will read about people who lived long ago.

2 We will not focus our attention on gods or goddesses.

3 These people were poor people or prisoners of war in most cases.

4 We will learn about a blood sport, which today many people consider to be barbaric.

Concept Map

Facts we already know about the **gladiators of Rome,** and the new facts we have learned

Gladiators of Rome

Integrating Ancient Civilizations with Reading Instruction © 2002 Creative Teaching Press

Word Warm-Up

Which words might you expect to find in a story about the **gladiators of Rome?**

barbaric	amphitheater	prominent
spectacle	trident	festivals
conquered	sacrifice	philosophers
machines	morality	tigers

Gladiators of Rome

A visitor to Rome today would witness the remains of many landmarks of the ancient Roman Empire. There is the Roman Forum. It was where the Roman government would hold its public meetings. Another landmark relic is the Pantheon. It was a temple built to honor the Roman gods. There is the Coliseum. This amphitheater was built by the Emperor Titus in A.D. 80 to house public sporting events.

The Roman poet Juvenal once said that all the people wanted was bread and games. Roman officials tried to appeal to the people by making sure they had grain for bread. They also offered large public festivals and sporting events. Many of these festivals and events took place throughout the year. By far, the most popular of these events were the gladiator games, oftentimes called blood games. These games were of three types: man against man, man against animal, and animal against animal. In man-against-man events, two men fought each other with various weapons. In man-against-animal events, an animal was pitted against a man who may or may not be armed. In animal-against-animal events, two wild animals fought each other. These animals were often exotic species. In all three cases, the fight was to the death.

The gladiators were the superstars of these games. Gladiator combat had a religious origin. At first, gladiators fought each other upon the death of a prominent man. The death of one or both men served as a human sacrifice. Only later did gladiator combat become a sport.

Gladiators were often prisoners of war, people taken from the conquered enemies of Rome. Convicted criminals sometimes served out a sentence as gladiators. Other gladiators were poor men with little chance of a comfortable life. Sometimes slaves were rented to participate in this sport. This practice was eventually banned. Finally, other gladiators were just plain thrill-seekers who

Integrating Ancient Civilizations with Reading Instruction © 2002 Creative Teaching Press

wanted adventure. There was always the promise of fame and fortune for a successful gladiator. Most often, gladiators met with a wretched death.

Gladiator schools were founded to turn these men into gladiators. These schools housed and fed the men as they prepared for the sports. Trainers, who were often former gladiators themselves, turned the men into fighting machines. The costumes and weapons of the gladiators were selected to add to the drama of the contests. Swords, tridents (3-pronged spears), nets, and body armor were used in various combinations. A heavily armed man fighting against a lightly armed man was always a favorite with the crowd.

When the contest began, the gladiators would enter and circle the arena. Once around, they would stop in front of the high official overseeing the event. The gladiators would then call out, "We who are about to die, salute you." Then the first event would begin. When it became obvious that one of the gladiators would shortly be defeated, he would look to the emperor and the crowd for confirmation of his final fate. If the emperor gave him a thumbs-up, he was shown mercy and allowed to live. If he received a thumbs-down, it meant death. Sometimes the opinion of the crowd could influence the decision of the emperor. A successful gladiator was rewarded with money and great fame. Occasionally, he was set free after a series of wins. Sometimes a gladiator could buy his freedom. Some even would return to the arena to fight again.

To modern society, these games seem to be a barbaric practice. The Roman citizens did not feel this way. They felt that these were men who had been condemned to death anyway. They held no pity for them. They were even less concerned about the animals. Some of the Roman philosophers did question the value or the morality of this violence. However, they were in the minority. These events got bigger and more spectacular every year. It was not long before entire battle scenes were staged. This required even bigger arenas. It was becoming very expensive to stage these enormous events. Eventually, two things caused the gladiator games to disappear. One reason was the cost. It finally became too expensive to pay for the structures and costumes. The other reason was the influence of Christianity. Christianity was a new religion that was quickly gaining in popularity. It was opposed to the killing of other human beings and the spectacle of the sport.

Comprehension Questions

? Literal Questions

1. What was a gladiator? Where did the gladiator games originate?
2. Why or how did people become gladiators?
3. What kind of training was available for gladiators?
4. What landmarks are still standing in Rome today?
5. What were the different types of gladiator games? How did they end?

? Inferential Questions

1. Why do you think emperors enjoyed watching the gladiator games?
2. Did gladiators have the option to quit fighting and/or competing? Why or why not?
3. The Roman poet Juvenal said, "All the people wanted was bread and games." What do you think this meant?
4. What do you think modern society thinks of the gladiator games? Why?
5. Why were humans and animals sacrificed?

? Making Connections

1. Does this story remind you of any television shows or movies? If so, which ones? Why?
2. Do we have our own versions of gladiator games? If so, what are they and how do they compare to the Romans' games?
3. Find out who some of the well-known gladiators were. Did any of them get out of the gladiator games? Where did most of these fights take place?
4. If you could travel back in time to see a gladiator game, would you want to? Why or why not?
5. In your opinion, which is the worst form of the gladiator games—man against man, man against animal, or animal against animal? Explain your thinking.

Integrating Ancient Civilizations with Reading Instruction © 2002 Creative Teaching Press

Sharpen Your Skills

1 What is the best synonym for the word "house" in this sentence?

This amphitheater was built by the Emperor Titus in A.D. 80 to **house** public sporting events.

- ○ home
- ○ hold
- ○ container
- ○ empty

2 Which of the following sentences does <u>not</u> have subject-verb agreement?

- ○ Neither of the gladiators want to lose in a blood fight.
- ○ The emperor was the person who decided if the gladiator would live or die.
- ○ The blood sport is banned today.
- ○ The emperor, as well as the audience, was cheering throughout the fight.

3 What part of speech is the word "that" in the following sentence?

I want to read **that** book about gladiators.

- ○ adverb
- ○ appositive
- ○ interjection
- ○ modifier

4 In which sentence is the word "served" used in the same way as in the following sentence?

Convicted criminals sometimes **served** out a sentence as a gladiator.

- ○ Have you served the ham yet?
- ○ She served as the president of the student body.
- ○ The volleyball player served the ball.
- ○ He served cookies at the tea party.

5 Which words would finish this analogy?

Boxers are to _____ as **gladiators** are to _____.

- ○ field/court
- ○ ring/contest
- ○ ring/Coliseum
- ○ contest/winning

6 How do you split the word "gladiators" into syllables?

- ○ gl-a-diat-ors
- ○ g-l-a-di-at-ors
- ○ gl-ad-i-a-tors
- ○ gla-di-a-tors

7 Which of the following sentences has the correct use of the irregular verb?

- ○ If you lived back then, would you have took pictures?
- ○ If you lived back then, would you had taken pictures?
- ○ If you lived back then, would you had took pictures?
- ○ If you lived back then, would you have taken pictures?

Name _____ Date _____

Jonathon has read many books about gladiators. He just got a new DVD player, so he rented a movie about a gladiator. At five different times during the movie, he stopped to tell his friend information he remembered reading about. Use the clues below to decide the order of the topics he commented on during the movie.

Clues

❶ The last comment he made was not related to any relics still present in Rome or the rulers who watched the events.

❷ His first comment was related to the fight between the two people. He was telling his friend about how they prepared for the battles.

❸ Jonathon said, "I know what those activities are called!" He said this after he mentioned the training process.

❹ His fourth comment was, "How did they live with themselves after showing a thumbs-down?"

❺ His last comment was, "I am so glad that I did not live back then. I would never have wanted to be one of those!"

	First comment	Second comment	Third comment	Fourth comment	Fifth comment
Gladiator Games					
Emperors					
Gladiators					
Landmarks					
Training					

Jonathon's first comment was about _____.

Jonathon's second comment was about _____.

Jonathon's third comment was about _____.

Jonathon's fourth comment was about _____.

Jonathon's fifth comment was about _____.

Integrating Ancient Civilizations with Reading Instruction © 2002 Creative Teaching Press

Gladiator Poem

Purpose

The purpose of this activity is for students to gain a greater understanding of gladiators and their thoughts and feelings. Students will write a Bio Poem about a gladiator they create in their mind.

MATERIALS

✔ Bio Poem Frame (page 72)
✔ copy of "Gladiators of Rome" story (pages 66–67)
✔ map of the Roman Empire
✔ plain white paper
✔ black pens
✔ colored pencils

Implementation

Explain to students that the Roman Empire covered an immense area at its height of power. When looking at a map of Europe, the empire completely covered the area surrounding the Mediterranean Sea. Many areas cooperated with Rome and a mutually beneficial relationship was agreed upon. However, some areas resisted Rome and wars were fought. The captives of these wars were often used as combatants in the gladiator games. Have students reread the story, and then discuss with the class the many feelings gladiators may have had, from fear to pride. Display a map of the Roman Empire, and have students help you list all the places that gladiators may have come from (e.g., North Africa, Spain, Britain). Give each student a Bio Poem Frame. Have students use the frame to write a "mini-biography" for a gladiator. Ask them to check their poem for spelling errors. Then, invite students to rewrite their poem on plain white paper. Have them use a black pen to outline their writing and use colored pencils to draw pictures to create a border around their poem. Encourage students to draw the weapons gladiators used, the places they came from, the arenas they fought in, and the gladiators themselves. Display the completed poems on a bulletin board, or bind them together in a class book.

General Bio Poem Example

President Bush
Brave, Compassionate, Angry, Motivated
Related to Barbara Bush
Who feels a need for justice
Who finds happiness in "The Land of the Free"
Who needs help from other countries
Who fears people destroying America
Who would like to see freedom for all
Who enjoys spending time serving fellow Americans
Who accomplished uniting several countries under a common cause
Who wishes for terrorism to end
A resident of Texas, U.S.A.
President of the United States of America

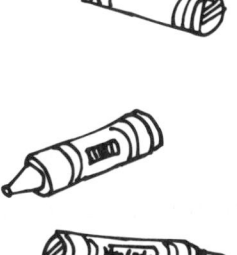

Bio Poem Frame

Line 1–(Name or Subject)– _____

Line 2–(Four Traits)– _____

Line 3–Related to _____

Line 4–Who feels _____

Line 5–Who finds happiness in _____

Line 6–Who needs _____

Line 7–Who fears _____

Line 8–Who would like to see _____

Line 9–Who enjoys _____

Line 10–Who accomplished _____

Line 11–Who wishes for _____

Line 12–A resident of _____

Line 13–(Nickname)– _____

General Bio Poem Example
President Bush
Brave, Compassionate, Angry, Motivated
Related to Barbara Bush
Who feels a need for justice
Who finds happiness in "The Land of the Free"
Who needs help from other countries
Who fears people destroying America
Who would like to see freedom for all
Who enjoys spending time serving fellow Americans
Who accomplished uniting several countries under a common cause
Who wishes for terrorism to end
A resident of Texas, U.S.A.
President of the United States of America

Integrating Ancient Civilizations with Reading Instruction © 2002 Creative Teaching Press